YOU'RE REA**
WRONG

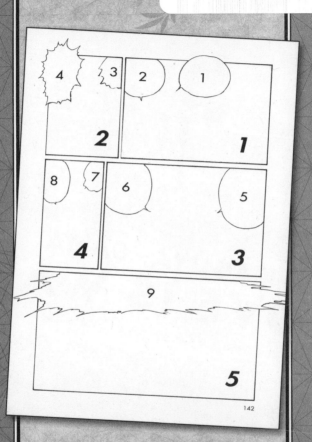

DEMON SLAYER: KIMETSU NO YAIBA
reads from right to left, starting in the
upper-right corner. Japanese is read from
right to left, meaning that action, sound
effects and word-balloon order are com-
pletely reversed from English order.

**Two geniuses. Two brains.
Two hearts. One battle.
Who will confess their love first...?!**

KAGUYA - SAMA
LOVE IS WAR

STORY & ART BY AKA AKASAKA

As leaders of their prestigious academy's student council, Kaguya and Miyuki are the elite of the elite! But it's lonely at the top... Luckily for them, they've fallen in love! There's just one problem—they both have too much pride to admit it. And so begins the daily scheming to get the object of their affection to confess their romantic feelings first...

Love is a war you win by losing.

KAGUYA-SAMA WA KOKURASETAI~TENSAITACHI NO REN'AI ZUNO SEN~
© 2015 by Aka Akasaka/SHUEISHA Inc.

viz.com

Dr. STONE

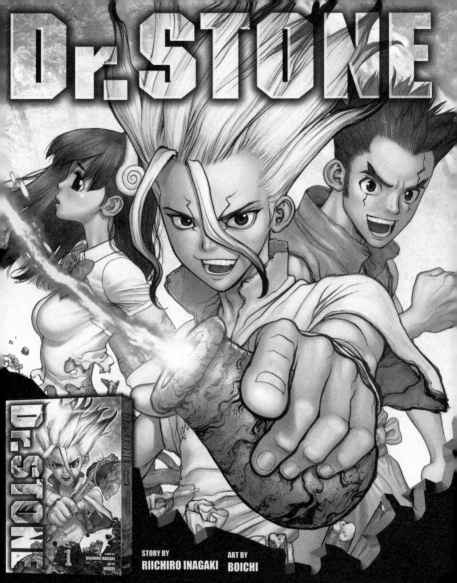

STORY BY
RIICHIRO INAGAKI

ART BY
BOICHI

One fateful day, all of humanity turned to stone. Many millennia later, Taiju frees himself from petrification and finds himself surrounded by statues. The situation looks grim—until he runs into his science-loving friend Senku! Together they plan to restart civilization with the power of science!

VOLUME 12—THE UPPER RANKS GATHER (THE END)

TANJIRO AND EVEN TOKITO DIDN'T KNOW IT WAS A DEMON UNTIL THEY SAW IT.

WHAT WAS SHOCKING WAS ITS SKILL AT REMAINING HIDDEN.

PERHAPS THEY HELD BACK BECAUSE THEY COULDN'T SEE A NUMBER IN ITS EYES...

...BUT THERE WAS NO DOUBT IT WAS AN UPPER-RANK DEMON.

MIST BREATHING

...TOKITO AND TANJIRO BOTH ASSUMED BATTLE STANCES.

IN LESS THAN THE TIME IT TAKES TO BLINK...

FOURTH FORM:

YES. VERY STRANGE. WHAT IS IT? I CAN'T FIND THE WORDS.

HUH?

STRANGE?

THAT GIRL IS A STRANGE CREATURE.

GRRR

HAS TAMAYO'S CAT COME BACK?

ACK!

UH-OH!

SHE WAS RESEARCHING THE CHANGE IN NEZUKO'S BLOOD AGAIN.

Umm...

AND IT WAS THAT WAY THEN TOO.

I'VE MET THAT GIRL BEFORE.

WHAT IS IT EXACTLY...?

YES.

HMM? IS SOMEONE HERE?

IT WON'T COME OUT IN FRONT OF TOKITO...

HUH?

OUCH!

HUH?

I SAID IT'S PERFECT!

BONK

NOW...

WHAT?

JUST NOW...

WHAT DID YOU JUST SAY?

LET'S GO FIND HAGANE-ZUKA TOGETHER.

...

...

GRRR

WAAH!

NEZUKO! YOU'RE UP!

Ow...

SHALL WE SEARCH TOGETHER?

KANAMORI IS MY NEW SWORD-SMITH.

WHERE IS HAGA-NEZUKA?

I KNOW KANAMORI. BUT WHY?

I'D GUESS HE'S WITH HAGANEZUKA.

HELPING OTHERS...

...OFTEN ENDS UP HELPING YOURSELF.

DON'T YOU HAVE YOUR OWN CON-CERNS?

...

WHY ARE YOU SO HELPFUL?

BESIDES, I WAS THINKING ABOUT DOING IT ANYWAY. SO THIS IS PERFECT.

SNORK!

DO YOU KNOW A SWORD-SMITH NAMED KANAMORI?

NUH-UH! IF YOU'D DONE IT IN ANGER I'D HAVE KNOWN!

BUT I WOULDN'T PINCH A NOSE IN ANGER.

ARGH!

YES.

AND YOU REACTED TOO SLOWLY.

SHWF

WAH! TOKITO!

DID YOU JUST PINCH MY NOSE?

CHAPTER 106:
ENEMY ATTACK

HMM ...?

I HAVE TO WORK EARLY IN THE MORNING.

I RELAXED IN THE BATH TOO LONG.

CLONK
CLONK
CLONK
CLONK
CLONK

A VASE?

WHO PUT A VASE OUT HERE?

IT COULD GET BROKEN.

THESE RICE CRACKERS ARE TASTY. WANT ONE?

GRAH!

SMASH

NO! GET LOST!

WASN'T YOUR FRONT TOOTH MISSING? AT THE HOT SPRING...?

HUH?

YOUR TOOTH...

YOU MUST BE MISTAKEN.

WHP

...

APPARENTLY, IT WILL TAKE THREE DAYS AND THREE NIGHTS FOR HAGANEZUKA TO POLISH THAT SWORD.

THAT HAPPENED YESTERDAY.

HE SAID THAT THE SHARPENING METHOD IS SO INCREDIBLY DEMANDING THAT IT'S KILLED PEOPLE.

HE'LL FINISH IT THE DAY AFTER TOMORROW.

I'M WORRIED.

...BUT MAY I GO SEE?

HE FORBADE ME FROM PEEKING IN...

...AND POLISH IT USING THE NICHIRIN SWORD POLISHING ART OF THE HAGANEZUKA FAMILY.

I WILL TAKE THIS TARNISHED KATANA...

GAH GAH

HIS SIDES!

HIS SIDES!

HIS SIDES!

WE DIDN'T TRUST YOU AND ALL YOU'D SAY WAS, "LEAVE IT TO ME!"

LIKE SOME IDIOT WHO CAN ONLY SAY ONE THING!

YOU SHOULD HAVE SAID SO FROM THE START!

PWAAAH

FOR ME...?

YES. SO HE CAN CREATE A STRONGER BLADE SO YOU WON'T DIE.

HE WON'T ADMIT THAT, THOUGH.

TRAINING?

NOD

NOD

TOSS POINK

FLOMP

MOST SWORDS-MEN DETEST HIM, SO HE ISN'T IN CHARGE OF THE SAME ONES FOR VERY LONG.

OH REALLY?

YOU'VE BEEN GETTING SWORDS FROM HIM FOR A LONG TIME...

...AND I THINK HE WAS HAPPY ABOUT THAT.

OH... ...HE'S BACK.

BOING

THAT'S WHY HE NEVER GOT MARRIED.

HIS INTER-PERSONAL SKILLS SUCK!

BLUNT

HYA
HA
HA
HA
HA!

BOYS! HAGANEZUKA'S WEAK SPOT IS HIS SIDES!

RIGHT HERE!

TICKLE

TICKLE

TICKLING HAGANEZUKA IMMOBILIZES HIM FOR A WHILE.

NOD

NOD

IT'S BEEN AWHILE, TANJIRO.

FLOMP

LET ME EXPLAIN.

LONG TIME NO SEE!

OH!

KANA-MORI!

HE WAS SECLUDED IN THE MOUNTAINS FOR TRAINING.

NOD

NOD

PLEASE, FORGIVE HAGANEZUKA.

WHO IS THAT?

HAGANE-ZUKA?!

WAAAAH!

LEAVE *WHAT* TO YOU?!

GWOOO

I HEARD EVERY-THING.

LEAVE IT TO ME!

HE LOOKED STRONGER THAN TANJIRO AFTER TRAINING...

...AND TRIED TO TAKE THE SWORD, SO THE THREE QUARRELED.

HAGANEZUKA SUDDENLY APPEARED, BULGING WITH MUSCLES.

SORRY TO DASH YOUR HOPES...

OF COURSE! IT'S BEEN THREE CENTURIES SINCE ANYONE CARED FOR IT.

IT'S TARNISHED...

TANJIRO...

WHOA! TANJIRO!

IT'S ALL RIGHT... I DON'T MIND.

I APOLOGIZE!

N-NO WAY! I BETTER NOT!

No, I can't do that!

ALL THE BATTLES IT'S BEEN THROUGH TOOK THEIR TOLL. IT JUST HAPPENED TO BREAK WHILE I WAS TRAINING WITH IT!

M-MAYBE IT'S OKAY FOR YOU TO TAKE IT!

YEAH... YOU SHOULD DEFINITELY TAKE IT!

STEEL FROM THE SENGOKU PERIOD IS HIGH QUALITY! TAKE IT!

BUT, BUT... YOU... BUT!

BUT YOU JUST HAPPEN TO BE IN TROUBLE BECAUSE YOU CAN'T GET A NEW SWORD FORGED, RIGHT?

IT'S ALL RIGHT! AS THE OWNER, I SAY SO!

ARE YOU *SURE* IT'S OKAY?!

KNCH

WOO-HOO

B-DMP

B-DMP

WANNA TRY PULLING IT OUT?

YEAH, I WANNA SEE IT!

CHAPTER 105:
SOMETHING
CAME OUT

From *Shonen Jump GIGA*, Winter Vol. 2, 2018

From *Weekly Shonen Jump*, combined
issue No. 21-22, 2018

HE WAS NOW ABLE TO TELL BY SMELL WHERE HIS OPPONENT WOULD AIM NEXT.

No more!

More please.

TANJIRO HAD AWAKENED...

...WITH THE ABILITY TO PREDICT MOVEMENTS.

...BUT THIS POWERFUL WEAPON GAVE HIM MOVEMENT COMPARABLE TO A HASHIRA'S.

TANJIRO'S BODY WAS STILL IMMATURE AND HIS REFLEXES WERE SLOWER THAN A HASHIRA'S...

THIS SMELL CAME TO HIM EARLIER THAN THE OPENING THREAD.

SPLOOSH

...AND HE FELL INTO THE RIVER.

IT FELT LIKE PEOPLE WERE MASSAGING HIM.

RUB

PAT

PAT

THE RIVER WAS DARK AND HEAVY...

...AND WARM FOR SOME REASON.

...THE SHINY ROCK HAD A SMELL EVEN UNDER THE WATER.

AS THE HANDS MASSAGED HIM, HE WENT TO GRAB IT.

AND ODDLY...

GLANCING AT THE RIVER-BED, HE SAW SOMETHING SHINY.

...VERY LITTLE WATER...

BUT WITH THAT FEAR-SOME AMOUNT OF EXER-CISE...

...AND NO FOOD...

...OR SLEEP...

GRAAAH

TANJIRO'S LIFE WAS SAVED BY THE FACT THAT IT STARTED RAINING.

...BEGAN TO CROSS THE RIVER TO THE AFTERLIFE.

...TAN-JIRO...

BUT HE WAS DIZZY FROM HUNGER...

FWFF

...HE WAS CROSS-ING THE BRIDGE.

WITH AN INDESCRIB-ABLE GIDDY FEELING...

AAAAAGH!

KNCH

NO FOOD AGAIN TODAY!

I COULD REALLY DIE EVEN WITH THOSE PRACTICE SWORDS!

WHEEZE

NO!

WHEEZE

HE DIDN'T KNOW THE LIMITS OF THE HUMAN BODY, SO HIS STYLE OF TRAINING WAS TERRIBLY HARSH.

C'MON!

WAIT A SECOND!

PLEASE, STAND UP!

C'MON, STAND UP!

KOTETSU HAD IMPRESSIVE POWERS OF ANALYSIS...

...BUT HE HAD NO SKILL IN TEACHING SWORDSMANSHIP.

HANG IN THERE! DON'T LOSE!

STAND UP!

I'M GONNA DIE!

STAND UP!

Unclouded eyes. →

THIS WAS TORTURE...

...BORN OF IGNORANCE!

WITHOUT WATER HUMANS WILL DIE IN THREE DAYS.

GIVE ME WATER!

NO!

JUST WATER...

IT WAS INHUMANE TO DENY TANJIRO FOOD AND WATER IF HE COULDN'T DO AS HE WAS TOLD.

NO!

WATER... NO!

KOTETSU...

I'M GONNA DIE.

IT WON'T OPEN UNLESS YOU MOVE IT THE RIGHT WAY.

IT'S JUST LIKE THAT.

YES, I KNOW WHAT IT IS. MY LITTLE SISTER HANAKO HAD ONE.

HAVE YOU EVER SEEN A *YOSEGI-ZAIKU* PUZZLE BOX?

YAY

I made this one.

You made that? Wow!

SWIP

KRK KRK

KRIK

OTHERWISE, THERE'D BE NO POINT IN USING IT FOR COMBAT TRAINING.

THE SWORDSMITHS DESIGNED IT WITH MOVEMENTS TO EXPLOIT THE WEAKNESSES OF SWORDSMEN.

IN THE CASE OF THIS DOLL, YOU CAN SET ITS ACTIONS BY THE NUMBER OF TIMES YOU TURN THE WRIST AND FINGERS.

SO *THE MECHANISM IS ONLY EFFECTIVE WITH INPUT FROM ITS OWNER.*

IN THE END, TOKITO WASTED HIS TIME.

...I'D DIE BEFORE I TOLD *THAT* TO ANYONE I HATED!

EVEN WITHOUT TRAINING TO RESIST TORTURE...

HEE HEE HEE

IT TURNED OUT KOTETSU HAD A GOOD EYE FOR ANALYZING FIGHTING STYLES.

BUT TOKITO'S ACTIONS SNAPPED HIM OUT OF IT.

HE WAS SO DEPRESSED BY HIS FATHER'S DEATH THAT HIS TONGUE FELL SILENT.

HE UNDERSTOOD THAT PEOPLE ARE OFTEN MOTIVATED BY ANGER.

Giyu

...AND WAS DISAPPOINTED...

...DESPITE BEING ONLY TEN YEARS OLD.

WITH HIS EXCELLENT POWERS OF OBSERVATION, HE CORRECTLY DIAGNOSED HIS WEAKNESS IN TECHNICAL ABILITY...

...ON THE BACK OF THE DOLL'S HEAD, YOU CAN CHANGE ITS MOVEMENTS.

Hmm?

I NEVER TOLD HIM THIS, BUT...

...IF YOU TURN THE KEY...

SLAP SLAP SLAP

DO YOUR BEST! I'LL SAY IT AGAIN, SO LISTEN UP!

YOU'RE USELESS IF THIS IS ALL IT TAKES TO KILL YOU!

Don't lose!

YANK

THE DOLL HAS FEWER MOVES NOW!

HE ONLY HAS FIVE ARMS BECAUSE THAT PUNK BROKE ONE!

YOU'RE MOVING BASED ON HABIT, TANJIRO. DON'T WATCH YOUR OPPONENT AND DECIDE WHAT YOU'LL DO BEFORE MOVING. THAT'S NO GOOD. UNDERSTAND? YOU'RE LACKING IN THE BASIC FUNDAMENTALS. I'M SURPRISED YOU SURVIVED THIS LONG. IN THE DEMON SLAYER CORPS, EVERYTHING IS DANGEROUS. I'LL BEAT THE WEAKNESSES OUT OF YOU! I WON'T GIVE YOU ANY FOOD UNTIL YOU CAN DO WHAT I'M TELLING YOU!

GACK

GRIP

KOTETSU ACTUALLY HAS A VENOMOUS TONGUE.

RIGHT...

"COMMIT SEPPUKU! YOU'RE SHAMELESS!"

"YOUR HAIR IS TOO LONG! LOOKS LIKE SEAWEED!"

"SHRIMP!"

"UGLY MIDGET!"

"IS THAT ALL YOU GOT, DIRTBAG?"

CHAPTER 104: KOTETSU

AND THEN TELL THAT GUY...

PLEASE GET STRONG, TANJIRO.

HE'S SMALLER AND YOUNGER THAN I AM, BUT...

... TOKITO WAS INCREDIBLE!

EVEN IF I DON'T VOICE IT...

NO! I CAN'T SAY SUCH HARSH THINGS!

MAYBE JUST HANG HIM?

NO! KOTETSU?!

I DON'T THINK...

NO!

BUT YOU WILL.

I MUST GET STRONGER TOO!

JUST SAY IT, OKAY?

...I WON'T BE BEATEN!

TANJIRO!

It's been a while!

By Mitsuri

Big Hand Cat. In addition to its big hands, this cat is distinctive for its fuzzy eyebrows and outie belly button.

Mitsuri Kanroji (19). Graduate of Kimetsu Academy. Currently she is attending a local art college. She's popular with the boys, but she hasn't noticed it, so she thinks she needs to search for a boyfriend.

My dream is making people all over the world happy through my art!!

LET'S GO LOOK...

...AND SEE IF IT STILL WORKS.

KOTETSU...

IT'S NOT MOVING.

...

SO I GUESS IT'S...

MOO

HMM.

KRK

KRK

KRIK

DISPOSE OF THAT.

WAH!

BONK

KTNK

I DON'T THINK HE DOES IT ON PURPOSE...

...BUT...

I DON'T SMELL ANY ANIMOS-ITY.

SWF

KAW

SWF

...

OH, THERE HE IS!

KOTETSU ...

KOTETSU ...

HMPH!

IT'S REALLY LOOKING DOWN ON ME...

...THAT CROW IS FULL OF ANIMOSITY!

MY SWORD BROKE, SO I'M TAKING THIS ONE.

KOTETSU!

SSWP

...!

SNIFF

...

OKAY.

LET'S WORK HARD TOGETHER!

GRIP

FWP

COMBAT TRAINING SHOULD LAST UNTIL DARK, SO I'LL GET READY TO SEE THIS TO THE END...LIKE I SHOULD.

I HOPED THE DOLL WOULD NEVER BREAK, BUT I'M DETERMINED.

TMP

MY LITTLE BROTH-ER—

YOU'RE TEN YEARS OLD?

UH-HUH.

TMP

TMP

OH!

EVEN IF YOU NEVER CAN DO IT, MAYBE YOUR CHILDREN OR GRANDCHILDREN WILL BE ABLE TO, RIGHT?

Get lost, you and your ugly eyelashes!

What're you lookin' at, low ranker?!

YOU HAVE TO PUT IN THE EFFORT FOR WHAT COMES NEXT.

EVEN IF YOU CAN'T DO IT YOURSELF, YOU'LL FIND SOMEONE ELSE TO CARRY ON FOR YOU.

GRAAH!

STILL, I BELIEVE THAT SOMEONE WILL ULTIMATELY GET IT DONE.

...AND HELP MY LITTLE SISTER WHO WAS TURNED INTO A DEMON.

I WANT TO DEFEAT MUZAN KIBUTSUJI...

AS SURELY AS SOMEONE SAVED OUR LIVES AND WE WENT ON TO DEFEAT AN UPPER-RANK DEMON...

BUT I MAY DIE BEFORE I ACCOMPLISH ANYTHING.

...THE LIVES WE SAVE ARE CERTAIN TO EVENTUALLY DEFEAT KIBUTSUJI.

...

EVENTUALLY YOU'LL BE ABLE TO DO ALL SORTS OF THINGS YOU CAN'T DO NOW!

YOU HAVE TO WORK HARD NOW SO YOU CAN BECOME THE PERSON YOU'LL BE IN TEN OR 20 YEARS!

YOUR FUTURE IS BRIGHT!

IT WILL ALL END WITH MY GENERATION AND IT'S MY FAULT!

NO, I WON'T!

I KNOW MYSELF! I'M JUST NO GOOD!

...

HE MOVED SILENTLY. THIS IS A SWORDS-MAN!

YOU CAN'T ABANDON YOUR RESPON-SIBILITY.

I DON'T WANT YOU TO TALK ABOUT YOURSELF LIKE THAT.

HUH? YOW!

KOTETSU!

WHSH

SNIFF SNIFF

KOTETSU!

KOTE—

But I'm not in good condition right now...

I'LL FIND YOU! I'VE GOT A GOOD NOSE!

KOTETSU!

I'LL HELP WITH THE DOLL IF THERE'S ANYTHING I CAN DO!

YOU CAN'T GIVE UP!

WOW! YOU'RE CLIMBING AT FULL SPEED, KOTETSU!

HIS ARMOR ...!

AAH!

Hmph!

...OR REMEMBER SOMETHING THEY HAVEN'T YET EXPERIENCED...

...AND WE CALL THAT AN INHERITED MEMORY.

THE FIRST TIME THEY MAKE A SWORD, THEY MIGHT REMEMBER SEEING A SIMILAR SCENE...

LIVING CREATURES CAN ALSO INHERIT MEMORIES.

I'M TANJIRO. WHAT'S YOUR NAME?

THAT'S KIND OF YOU. THANK YOU.

KEH!

THAT'S A FANTASY!

FAAAN-TASYYY!

THE DREAM YOU HAD MUST HAVE BEEN AN ANCESTOR'S MEMORY!

SKRAKK

NEVER MIND THAT MEAN LADY CROW.

I'M KOTETSU.

DO YOU KNOW A WARRIOR FROM THE SENGOKU PERIOD? HOW OLD ARE YOU?

WHAT ARE YOU DOING IN THIS VILLAGE? THAT'S SO UNREALISTIC I COULD LAUGH!

WHAT? ARE YOU STUPID?!

S- SORRY. I'M STRANGE, AREN'T I?

NO, NO!

SHMP

KEH!

PEOPLE IN OUR VILLAGE TALK ABOUT THAT!

FAMILIES PASS ON MORE THAN JUST THEIR OUTWARD APPEARANCE.

MAYBE IT'S AN *INHERITED MEMORY!*

TEE HEE HEE HEE!

HMPH!

HMMPH!

HMPH!

HE'S A GENIUS!

HE'S ON A WHOLE DIFFERENT LEVEL THAN YOU LOT!

BUT HE DOESN'T USE SUN BREATHING, RIGHT?

IS HE REALLY THAT INCREDIBLE?

ARE YOU TOKITO'S CROW? BY SUN BREATHING, YOU MEAN THE ORIGINAL STYLE OF BREATHING?

I SAW THAT PERSON IN A DREAM!

GASP

I REMEMBER! IT WAS A DREAM!

GYAAAH!

SHUT UP! I'LL PECK OUT YOUR EYES!

SO THAT'S WHY YOU'RE SO...

I SEE...

I SEE...

TREMBLE

I HAVE TO DO A GOOD JOB...

MY FATHER DIED SUDDENLY AND I DON'T HAVE ANY SIBLINGS.

...BUT I HAVE NO TALENT WITH SWORDS OR MECHANICAL THINGS.

SHAKE

HE ISN'T THAT MUCH OLDER THAN ME, BUT HE'S A HASHIRA... HE HAS TALENT...

HE'S...

...INCREDIBLE.

?!

THAT BOY DESCENDS FROM USERS OF SUN BREATHING!

OF COURSE!

HURM

HMM

SORRY, BUT I DON'T KNOW MUCH ABOUT IT.

IT WAS DURING THE SENGOKU PERIOD.

I FEEL LIKE I KNOW HIM, BUT I'M NOT SURE.

WHO WAS THAT SWORDSMAN? WHERE WAS HE FROM AND WHAT DID HE DO?

THE DOLL HASN'T BROKEN ONCE IN ALL THAT TIME?

YOU MEAN... OVER 300 YEARS AGO?!

TH...

THE SENGOKU PERIOD?!

HUH?

IF IT BREAKS, WE CAN'T REPAIR IT.

IT'S AMAZING TECHNOLOGY THAT WE CAN'T MATCH EVEN TODAY.

I KNOW THAT.

I RECOGNIZE THAT FACE.

ITS ARMS...

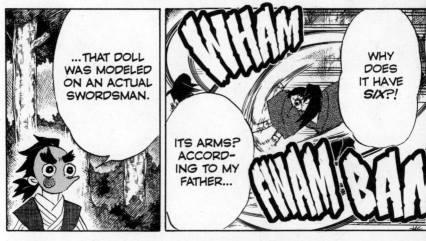

...THAT DOLL WAS MODELED ON AN ACTUAL SWORDSMAN.

WHY DOES IT HAVE SIX?!

ITS ARMS? ACCORDING TO MY FATHER...

WHAM

FWAM BAM

...IT COULDN'T RE-CREATE THAT SWORDSMAN'S MOVEMENTS.

HE SAID IF IT DIDN'T HAVE SIX ARMS...

CHAPTER 103: YORIICHI TYPE ZERO

A NEW EIGHT-PANEL COMIC: MITSURI'S CORPS UNIFORM

A MECHANI-CAL DOLL.

HMM?

MECHANI-CAL DOLL?

BUT THIS KEY... WHAT'S IT A KEY TO?

IT'S STRONGER THAN A HUMAN, SO WE USE IT FOR COMBAT TRAINING.

WHOARR!

REALLY?! THAT'S AMAZING!

YES.

MY ANCESTORS MADE IT AND IT CAN DO 108 MOVEMENTS.

TMP TMP

THIS WAY!

FWAM

WHOA! WHAT THE...?!

HE'S STARTED.

YES. BUT IT'S GETTING OLD AND MIGHT BREAK.

OH! HE WANTS TO TRAIN WITH IT?

I MEAN, WE COULDN'T DO ANYTHING IF WE DIDN'T HAVE ACTUAL SWORDS!

THE SWORD-SMITHS ARE IMPORTANT AND DO CRUCIAL WORK!

THEY'RE DIFFER-ENT FROM SWORDSMEN BUT THEY STILL HAVE INCREDIBLE SKILLS!

WE JUST EACH FIGHT IN OUR OWN PLACE!

SWORDS-MEN AND SWORD-SMITHS NEED EACH OTHER!

WE'RE BOTH PART OF THE FIGHT!

SORRY, BUT...

...I DON'T HAVE TIME FOR THIS POINTLESS CONVERSATION.

THAT'S WHAT IT MEANS TO INTERFERE WITH A HASHIRA.

?!

IF YOU USED YOUR HEAD JUST A LITTLE, YOU'D UNDERSTAND.

YOUR TIME AND A HASHIRA'S TIME HAVE COMPLETELY DIFFERENT VALUE.

SWORDSMITHS CAN'T FIGHT. THEY CAN'T SAVE SOMEONE'S LIFE. THEY ONLY HAVE THE ABILITY TO MAKE WEAPONS.

THE KEY!

SO COME ON...

TWITCH

EVEN IF THEY TORTURE ME! NEVER!

IT'LL BREAK NEXT TIME!

SHAKE

I...

I WON'T GIVE THE KEY TO ANYONE!

TREMBLE

YOU APPEAR TO BE AN EXCEEDINGLY DUMB BRAT.

EVEN MOST ADULTS CAN'T ENDURE IT, SO IT'S IMPOSSIBLE THAT YOU COULD.

HAVE YOU BEEN TRAINED TO WITH-STAND TORTURE?

WHILE YOU'RE RATTLING ON AND ON AND ON AND ON WITH YOUR NONSENSE...

...DO YOU KNOW HOW MANY PEOPLE WILL DIE?

SO WHAT IF IT DOES BREAK? WHY NOT MAKE IT AGAIN?

FWP

!

...

THROB

THROB

ARE YOU ALL RIGHT?

YOU MUST BE UPSET. THAT WAS CLOSE!

GO AWAY!

WSH

SHOVE

HEY...

LEMME GO!

HE GOT THE BOY...

UNGH!

LET GO OF—

WHAT ARE YOU DOING TO THAT CHILD?

WHO ARE YOU?

YOU'RE REALLY NOISY.

I CAN'T BUDGE HIM!

YOU LET GO.

BUT HIS ARMS ARE THIN AND HE'S SMALLER THAN ME!

RRGH...

AND I DEFINITELY WON'T TELL YOU HOW TO USE IT!

GET OUT OF HERE!

WHATEVER HAPPENS, I WON'T GIVE YOU THE KEY!

WHAT SHOULD I DO? EAVES-DROPPING IS RUDE.

BUT IF THEY'RE FIGHTING, I SHOULD STEP IN.

WHAT'S WRONG? ARE THEY FIGHTING?

?!

SWIP

WHAT DID SHINOBU CALL HIM...?

OH, RIGHT.

HMM? IF I REMEMBER, THAT'S A HASHIRA...

THE MIST HASHIRA.

...TOKITO.

MUICHIRO...

MAYBE A SWORD? MAYBE IT'S BURIED OR SOMETHING! THIS IS EXCITING! LIKE I'M ON A TREASURE HUNT!

HMM...

I WONDER WHAT WEAPON KANROJI WAS TALKING ABOUT.

HMM?

AND I WANT TO FIND HAGANE-ZUKA, BUT...

HMM... AND NOT BEING COMPLETELY HEALTHY IS HAMPERING MY NOSE.

THIS IS A REALLY GREAT PLACE, BUT THE HOT SPRING SMELL IS STRONG.

AND...

...WHO'S THAT...?

...

...

A CHILD?

I'LL TRY HARDER AND HARDER...

BUT I STILL HAVE A LONG WAY TO GO!

...TO BEAT MUZAN KIBUTSUJI HIMSELF!

UZUI JUST LET US WIN.

BDMP

SHWF

?

GLANCE

UH, YEAH. BASICALLY.

YOU GOT PERMISSION TO STAY A LONG TIME, RIGHT?

SHIFT

FIDGET

THAT'S AN INCREDIBLE EXPERIENCE.

YOU FOUGHT AN UPPER-RANK DEMON AND SURVIVED.

TANJIRO, YOU'RE MUCH STRONGER NOW THAN YOU WERE BEFORE.

WHAT YOU GAIN THROUGH ACTUAL EXPERIENCE IS MORE VALUABLE THAN ANYTHING.

IT'S COMPARABLE TO FIVE OR TEN YEARS OF TRAINING.

THANK YOU.

MITSURI KANROJI IS ROOTING FOR THE KAMADO SIBLINGS!

LOOKS LIKE I HAVE TO GO.

OH MY!

PLEASE, COME TO THE WORKSHOP FOR FINAL ADJUSTMENTS.

YOUR SWORD WILL SOON BE FINISHED BEING SHARPENED.

NO, I'LL PROBABLY LEAVE LATE AT NIGHT.

DON'T WORRY! I'LL SEE YOU OFF!

TANJIRO...

REALLY? HMM...

NO...

BUT...

...LET'S TRY OUR BEST TO DO SO!

...I DON'T KNOW IF WE'LL EVER SEE EACH OTHER ALIVE AGAIN, BUT...

I DON'T REALLY KNOW WHY, BUT I FIND BOTH THE SHINAZUGAWA BROTHERS SCARY.

TICKLE TICKLE

THERE ARE FIVE KIDS IN MY FAMILY, AND WE ALL GET ALONG.

MMPH MMPH

I WONDER WHY.

OH, REALLY?

PEEK

ONE OF THE VILLAGERS SAID HE DOESN'T TAKE MEALS AT ALL.

I DON'T THINK HE'LL COME.

MAYBE HE BROUGHT HIS OWN FOOD.

IT WOULD BE NICE TO TALK TO HIM AT LEAST A LITTLE.

GENYA HASN'T COME YET, HUH?

How cute!

HEY-YA-HEY-YA-HEY!

...SAYING CONQUER THE EMPEROR'S ENEMY!

DIDN'T YOU KNOW IT'S A BROCADE STANDARD...

YEAH! LET'S DO THAT!

I WONDER IF HE'S ALL RIGHT. I'LL TAKE HIM SOME RICE BALLS LATER.

GYAAH!

I'M GONNA EAT A LOT AND GET STRONG TOO!

BUT I DIDN'T EAT *THAT* MUCH TONIGHT.

REALLY?

YOU DON'T SAY!

OH!

KANROJI, THE BOY YOU MET AT THE HOT SPRING BECAME A DEMON SLAYER AT THE SAME TIME AS ME. HIS NAME IS GENYA SHINAZUGAWA.

OH YEAH...

MAYBE THEY'RE NOT ON GOOD TERMS. THAT'S TOO BAD.

BUT SHINAZUGAWA SAID HE DOESN'T HAVE A LITTLE BROTHER.

HE MUST BE SHINAZUGAWA'S LITTLE BROTHER.

! SOME-ONE LOST A TOOTH!

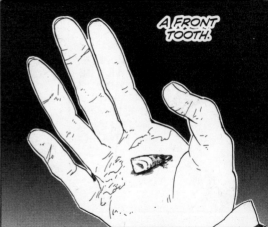

A FRONT TOOTH.

SUMI SAID HIS NAME IS...

That man is...

HIS HEAD IS SHAVED ON THE SIDES...!

WELL, SUPPER WILL BE READY SOON. I HEAR IT'LL BE RICE WITH MATSUTAKE MUSHROOMS.

SOB SOB SOB

THE CALM I GOT FROM SOAKING IS COMPLETELY SHATTERED!

WHOA! REALLY?!

PONK

OW!

WOW! IT'S HUGE!

AT THE HOT SPRING...

WHAT'S THAT FLAPPING IN FRONT OF THE HORSE?

♪ MIYA-SAN, MIYA-SAN!

SHE'S A BIG EATER!

TANJIROOO!

OHHH! IT'S TANJIRO!

HE IGNORED ME! I SAID HELLO, BUT HE IGNORED ME!

CARE-FUL!

LISTEN! LISTEN!

WAAAH

YOUR BOOBS ARE ABOUT TO SPILL OUT!

WATCH OUT!

WHOA, BE CAREFUL!

ISN'T THAT MEAN? I'M A HASHIRA!

WAAH

FLAP FLAP

I ASKED HIS NAME BUT HE IGNORED ME!

I DON'T KNOW!

WHO DID?

IF HOTARU DOESN'T FORGE YOU A SWORD BY THE TIME YOU'RE READY, I'LL APPOINT SOMEONE ELSE TO BE YOUR SWORDSMITH.

I HEARD YOU HAVEN'T YET RECOVERED ENOUGH TO GO DEMON SLAYING.

WELL, DON'T BE TOO ROUGH.

...SO JUST RELAX HERE.

OUR HOT SPRING IS VERY GOOD FOR HEALING THE BODY...

*SIGNS: BATH

I'LL BE DOWN HERE PREPARING YOUR MEAL.

THE HOT SPRING IS UP THIS HILL.

I HOPE THEY DON'T FIGHT.

TMP TMP

OKAY!

...THAT'S WRONG.

NO...

IT'S ALL BECAUSE I DO THINGS LIKE BREAK MY SWORD AND CHIP THE BLADE!

NO, NO, IT'S OKAY!

IT'S *HIS* FAULT FOR MAKING DULL BLADES THAT BREAK.

...SO DON'T WORRY.

WE'LL BRING HIM BACK AS SOON AS WE FIND HIM...

FWSH

GULP

ULP

...

WE'RE SEARCHING FOR HIM, SO PLEASE BE PATIENT.

IT SEEMS THAT HOTARU HAS DISAPPEARED.

VRRRR

THANK YOU!

WHAT A CUTE NAME!

I NAMED HIM.

YES... HOTARU HAGANEZUKA.

HOTARU?

HE THROWS TANTRUMS AND GOES OFF TO SULK.

HE'S BEEN THAT WAY SINCE HE WAS SMALL.

THAT'S SAD.

HE SAID IT WAS TOO CUTE AND GOT MAD AT ME.

SIGH

SORRY.

I'M THE CHIEF OF THIS VILLAGE— *TECCHIN TECCHI-KAWAHARA.*

NICE TO MEET YA.

GREET-INGS.

SO ESTEEMED THAT YOU SHOULD BOW TILL YOUR HEAD TOUCHES THE TATAMI MAT.

ZZWINK

I'M THE TOWN'S SMALLEST AND MOST ESTEEMED PERSON.

*A JAPANESE SNACK

COME. I'LL GIVE YOU SOME *KARINTO.*

OH, WHAT A NICE YOUNG MAN.

IT'S A PLEA-SURE TO MEET YOU!

BONK

I'M TANJIRO KAMADO!

BOW

IT'S LIKE THERE'S A HOT SPRING NEARBY!

WHAT INCREDIBLE BUILDINGS!

AND THIS SMELL ...

THERE *IS*.

THANK YOU VERY MUCH!

NOW I WILL TAKE MY LEAVE.

BOW

ALL RIGHT!

GO LEFT OVER THERE AND THAT WILL TAKE YOU TO THE CHIEF'S HOUSE. FIRST GO GREET HIM.

THANK YOU VERY MUCH!

THANK YOU VERY MUCH!

THANK YOU VERY MUCH!

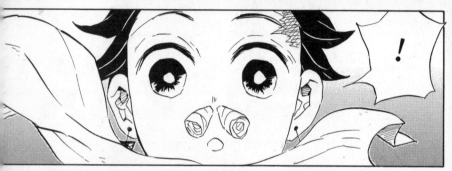

CROWS LEAD EACH KAKUSHI TO THE PLACE OF THE NEXT KAKUSHI, BUT THOSE CROWS OFTEN CHANGE AS WELL.

FURTHERMORE, THEY FREQUENTLY CHANGE THE ROUTES AND THE KAKUSHI ALONG THEM.

WHEW! SMART PEOPLE ARE AMAZING!

APPARENTLY, EVEN MORE COMPLICATED METHODS HIDE MASTER UBUYASHIKI'S MANSION.

TANJIRO SAID THIS EVERY TIME A KAKUSHI PASSED HIM ON, WHICH PLEASED THE KAKUSHI.

BLUSH   BLUSH

I'M COUNTING ON YOU!

THANK YOU!

GOOD WORK!

GUAH!

STUFF

ALSO, SINCE YOU HAVE A GOOD SENSE OF SMELL— NOSE PLUGS!

IN ORDER TO PREVENT DEMONS FROM ATTACKING THE VILLAGE, NO ONE KNOWS ITS LOCATION.

BEFORE PLUGGING MY EARS, SHE BRIEFLY EXPLAINED.

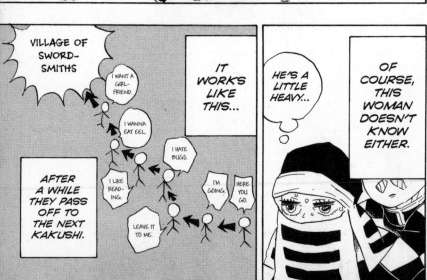

VILLAGE OF SWORD-SMITHS

I WANT A GIRL-FRIEND.

I WANNA EAT EEL

I HATE BUGS.

I LIKE READING.

I'M GOING.

HERE YOU GO.

LEAVE IT TO ME.

IT WORKS LIKE THIS...

AFTER A WHILE THEY PASS OFF TO THE NEXT KAKUSHI.

HE'S A LITTLE HEAVY...

OF COURSE, THIS WOMAN DOESN'T KNOW EITHER.

THE MASTER OF THE HOUSE GRANTED PERMISSION, SO I WILL GUIDE YOU.

PLEASED TO MEET YOU.

...BUT IT'S NICE TO MEET YOU.

NOW PUT THESE ON.

SWIP

BECAUSE OF WHERE I'M GUIDING YOU, I CAN-NOT NAME MYSELF...

I'M TANJIRO KAMADO! IT'S A PLEASURE!

BOW

NICE TO MEET YOU!

FURTHER-MORE, I WILL *CARRY* YOU THERE.

IT'S A HIDDEN VILLAGE.

A BLIND-FOLD AND EAR-PLUGS.

WHAT ARE THOSE?

HUH?

...BUT HAGANEZUKA CAN BE A BIT TOUCHY.

HMM...?

SWORDS OFTEN GET DAMAGED...

THE VILLAGE WITH ALL THE SWORD-SMITHS.

VILLAGE?

MAYBE IT WOULD BE BEST TO TALK TO HIM DIRECTLY.

HOW ABOUT GOING TO THE VILLAGE?

*THEY'RE EATING RICE CRACKERS.

HUH?

CAN I GO?

YEAH! ...BAD! THIS IS...

...BUT I BROKE IT ONCE BEFORE!

AHH... URGH...

THIS TIME IT JUST GOT CHIPPED...

O...

OHHH...

IT'S BEEN TWO MONTHS, BUT NO KATANA CAME...

URGH! HOW FRUSTRATING!

I CAN'T STRETCH OUT FLAT!

AS EXPECTED, MY PHYSICAL STRENGTH IS SLOW TO RETURN!

SMUSH KNEAD

KRIIIK

WAS A KATANA DELIVERED WHILE I WAS ASLEEP? MY SWORD GOT CHIPPED.

OH YEAH...

YANK

...YOU WANNA SEE?

DO...

A LETTER CAME FROM HAGANE-ZUKA.

KATANA? KATANA...?

ULP!

GACK

KANAO, LET'S GO MAKE SOME RICE GRUEL.

OKAY.

Aoi

PLEASE, BE QUIET!

DON'T SAY UNLUCKY THINGS!

OH NO! HE'S UN-CONSCIOUS AGAIN!

I HOPE HE RECOVERS QUICKLY AND CAN EAT A LOT.

STARE

THEY'RE ALL MONSTERS.

Letter from Kiyo.

WHOA, SERIOUSLY?

Camping out.

I'm the strongest!

INOSUKE WENT OUT ON A MISSION.

I'm the wind!

ONE WEEK LATER, TANJIRO WAS BACK ON HIS FEET.

I'm next!

I'm next!

TADAAAH

IT'S A WEASEL FROM ANOTHER COUNTRY CALLED A HONEY BADGER!

POISON DOESN'T AFFECT IT, SO IT EVEN FIGHTS POISONOUS SNAKES... AND EATS THEM!

It's cute.

Wow

ITS THICK SKIN IS LIKE ARMOR.

IT'S FINE EVEN IF A LION BITES IT!

MAYBE SHE GOT TIRED OF WORRYING ABOUT HIM?

...

LADY KOCHO CAN BE CARELESS.

HEH HEH...

SHINOBU SAID INOSUKE IS THE SAME WAY.

TEE HEE

GET DOWN HERE!

HE'S ACTIVE AGAIN. HE'S ON A MISSION, BUT RELUCTANTLY.

THE YELLOW-HEADED ONE... WAS IT TWO DAYS AGO?

ZENITSU WOKE UP THE NEXT DAY.

YEP!

THEY WERE *INCREDIBLY* SHOCKED.

ALL THE KAKUSHI WERE SHOCKED AT HOW DURABLE HE IS.

Agh! Ow! This is irritating!

THE SOUND HASHIRA WAS WALKING BUT LEANING ON HIS WIVES' SHOULDERS.

Crazy, isn't it? With those injuries!

He... he's standing! Scary!

THE POISON GOT DEEP IN HIM, SO HE WAS SLOW TO USE BREATHING TO STOP THE BLEEDING AND...

INOSUKE'S CONDITION WAS REALLY BAD.

OH... AND INOSUKE?

HE WAS IN DANGER FOR A WHILE TOO.

...IF IT LOOKS LIKE IT'S GOING BAD, YOU CAN THROW IT AWAY OR EAT IT...

UM, I'M PUTTING THE CASTELLA HERE...

...YOU...

THANK...

TH...

HE...

YOU SHOULD BE MORE EXCITED!

HE'S AWAKE ?!

IT'S A PRESENT FOR HIM, EVEN THOUGH HE STILL HASN'T REGAINED CONSCIOUSNESS.

AND WHAT I'M CARRYING IN MY HANDS IS FINE CASTELLA.

TO BE HONEST, IT'S TAKING ALL MY STRENGTH TO KEEP FROM EATING IT RIGHT NOW.

THEY'RE YOUNGER THAN I AM BUT THEY'RE SWORDSMEN WHO RISK THEIR LIVES FIGHTING—I TRULY RESPECT THEM!

I DON'T GET THIS GUY. →

VEEN

BROKEN VASE

CLEAN THIS UP!

THE DOOR IS OPEN.

I HEAR HE HAS A GOOD NOSE, SO IF I SET IT NEAR HIM MAYBE HE'LL WAKE UP.

BUT SHE OUTRANKS ME, SO I CAN'T SAY ANYTHING. EVEN THOUGH I'M 23.

KLNK

TNK

SHE'S A WEIRD GIRL. SHE DOESN'T TALK AT ALL. IT'S BECAUSE THEY MADE HER A DEMON SLAYER AT SUCH A YOUNG AGE.

SERIOUSLY, KANAO? SHE LEAVES EVERYTHING UNDONE!

I'M A KAKUSHI IN THE CLEAN-UP CREW OF THE DEMON SLAYER CORPS.

MY NAME IS GOTO.

I'M ALSO THE ONE WHO FOUND HIM AND THE OTHERS IN THE ENTERTAINMENT DISTRICT TWO MONTHS AGO.

TP TP

I HAVE A FATEFUL CONNECTION WITH HIM.

I'M THE ONE WHO TOLD TANJIRO KAMADO "HOW LONG ARE YOU GONNA SLEEP?! GET UP ALREADY, WOULD YA?!" DURING THE HASHIRA MEETING.

GRAH! YAH!

THAT'S WHAT I THOUGHT... BUT THEY WERE JUST UNCONSCIOUS.

THEY'RE SUCH CLOSE FRIENDS!

THEY LOOKED LIKE THIS.

CHAPTER 100:
GO TO THE
VILLAGE!

SINCE THE FIGHT, YOU'VE BEEN UNCON- SCIOUS FOR TWO MONTHS.

ARE YOU ALL RIGHT ?

...

...

OH... REALLY ?

I...

...WAS?

...THAT YOU'RE AWAKE.

I'M GLAD...

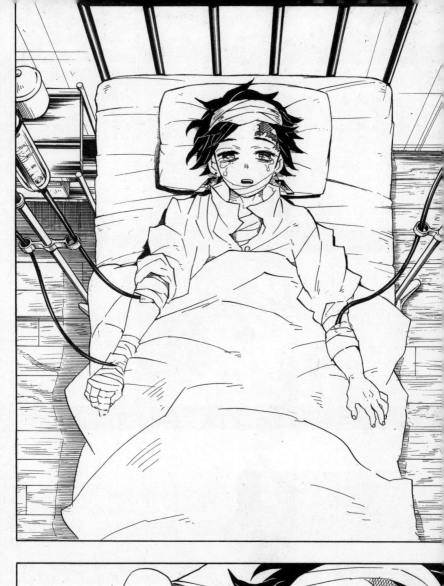

WHERE... AM I?

WAS THAT...A DREAM?

...AND I WAS UNABLE TO ACCOMPLISH EVEN ONE THING THAT I SHOULD HAVE IN THIS LIFE.

I CANNOT PROTECT ANYTHING THAT'S IMPORTANT TO ME...

AW...

PLEASE DON'T...

I AM A MAN WITHOUT ANY VALUE.

I BEG YOU, DON'T TALK ABOUT YOURSELF LIKE THAT.

PLEASE...

I DON'T WANT YOU TO TALK LIKE THAT.

SO VERY SAD.

IT'S SAD...

*SIGNS: PARADISE

NO ONE'S ANY FUN.

UGH...

I'M OVER-THINKING IT, AREN'T I, LORD AKAZA?

I SORTA FEEL LIKE I WAS CUT OUT OF THAT CONVERSATION.

LORD AKAZA! WE WERE STILL TALKING!

BW SH

FLOP FLIP

SEND ME AND HANTENGU TO THE SAME PLACE!

I'M DEFINITELY GOING TO KILL YOU.

...ENCOURAGEMENT.

YOU HAVE MY...

YES.

VWUSH

GOOD-BYE!

...

GOOD-BYE, LORD KOKUSHIBO!

*EYES: UPPER 1

CHAPTER 99:
SOMEONE'S DREAM

...WHEN THE INFORMATION IS CONFIRMED, GO THERE WITH HANTENGU.

GYOKKO...

SLAM

SHMP

LORD GYOKKO!

BUT I GOT THE INFORMATION!

...!

AS YOU WISH!

AIEEE!

OUTRAGEOUS! BUT THAT'S ALL RIGHT...

TK

CHK.

TWK

!

I DETEST *CHANGE*.

MOST CHANGES CAUSE WEAKNESS AND INFERIORITY.

CHANGING CIRCUMSTANCES... CHANGES OF THE FLESH...

...CHANGING EMOTIONS...

A PERFECT STATE... UNCHANGING FOREVER!

LORD MUZAN IS TOUCHING MY HEAD! SO VERY NICE!

I PREFER THE *UNCHANGING!*

...

FORGIVE US! PLEASE! PLEASE!

AIEEEE!

SO WHAT CAN I DO?

I'M NO GOOD AT DETECTIVE WORK.

UBU-YASHIKI...IS HIDING...

...SKILL-FULLY.

I HAVE...

...NO EXCUSES...

...TO MAKE.

JUST NOW I-

I HAVE INFORMATION TO BRING YOUR HOPES ONE STEP CLOSER!

I'M DIFFER-ENT!

LORD MUZAN!

BUT THAT'S FINE.

I DON'T EXPECT MUCH FROM YOU ANYWAY.

YOU'RE ALL WORTHLESS.

YOU'RE FALLING IN THE ORDER OF WHO HAS THE MOST HUMAN PARTS REMAINING.

YOU STILL HAVEN'T PUT THE UBUYASHIKI FAMILY IN ITS GRAVE.

AND THE *BLUE SPIDER LILY*...

HAVE I EVER FAILED TO MEET YOUR EXPECTATIONS?

YOU'RE SAYING SAD THINGS AGAIN.

...NO LONGER KNOW WHY YOU EVEN EXIST.

KR IKK

I...

AFTER HUNDREDS OF YEARS YOU STILL HAVEN'T FOUND IT.

...HOW SHALL I MAKE AMENDS? SHALL I GOUGE OUT AN EYEBALL OR...

I BROUGHT GYUTARO IN, SO...

MY APOLO-GIES!

CAN THAT REALLY BE SO?

YEAH

YEAH

YEAH

GRIN

I SUSPECTED GYUTARO WOULD LOSE. AS I THOUGHT, DAKI WAS A HINDRANCE.

THAT'S NOT NECESSARY. YOU MAY KEEP YOUR EYEBALLS.

...IT DOESN'T MATTER NOW.

HE SHOULDN'T HAVE FOUGHT AFTER POISONING THEM. BUT...

SKWIP

IF GYUTARO HAD FOUGHT BY HIMSELF FROM THE BEGINNING, HE WOULD HAVE WON.

SKWIP

!!

AIEEEE!

HE'S BEEN OVER THERE THE WHOLE TIME.

UPPER RANK 1 WAS CALLED FIRST.

*DOMA'S EYES: UPPER 2

DURING THE TIME WE DIDN'T MEET, GYOKKO BECAME UNCOUNTABLE IN NUMBER.

HOW HORRIBLE... HOW HORRIBLE...

AN INDIVISIBLE NUMBER... A STRANGE, OMINOUS NUMBER...

AN ODD NUMBER!

HOW HORRIBLE... HOW HORRIBLE!

IT'S BEEN 113 YEARS SINCE THE LAST SUMMONS.

UPPER RANK 4

HANTENGU

...IS LORD MUZAN HERE?

BIWA WOMAN...

*UPPER 3

CHAPTER 98:
THE UPPER RANKS
GATHER

CONTENTS

**THE
UPPER
RANKS
GATHER**

HAGANEZUKA

The swordsmith who made Tanjiro's katana. He has the soul of an artist, so he gets angry when a blade is treated poorly.

INOSUKE HASHIBIRA

He also went through Final Selection at the same time as Tanjiro. He wears the pelt of a wild boar and is very belligerent.

ZENITSU AGATSUMA

He went through Final Selection at the same time as Tanjiro. He's usually cowardly, but when he falls asleep his true power comes out.

MUZAN KIBUTSUJI

Kibutsuji turned Nezuko into a demon! He is Tanjiro's enemy and hides his nature in order to live among human beings.

KAGAYA UBUYASHIKI

The leader of the Demon Slayer Corps who seeks to defeat Muzan Kibutsuji. His body is weak, but he is very charismatic.

UPPER RANK 6 FROM OVER 100 YEARS AGO

The demon who turned Gyutaro and Daki—who were until recently the Upper Rank 6 demons—into demons.

AKAZA: UPPER RANK 3

Upper Rank 3. The demon who killed Kyojuro Rengoku, the Flame Hashira of the Demon Slayer Corps. He burns with desire for revenge against Tanjiro.

TANJIRO KAMADO

A kind boy who saved his sister and now aims to avenge his family. He can smell the scent of demons and an opponent's weakness.

Tanjiro's younger sister. A demon attacked her and turned her into a demon. But unlike other demons, she fights her urges and tries to protect Tanjiro.

NEZUKO KAMADO

STORY

In Taisho-era Japan, young Tanjiro makes a living selling charcoal. One day, demons kill his family and turn his younger sister Nezuko into a demon. Tanjiro and Nezuko set out to find a way to return Nezuko to human form and defeat Kibutsuji, the demon who killed their family!

After joining the Demon Slayer Corps, Tanjiro meets Tamayo and Yushiro—demons who oppose Kibutsuji—who provide a clue to how Nezuko may be turned back into a human. On a new mission, Uzui the Sound Hashira, Tanjiro and others confront a brother-and-sister pair of demons who are Upper Rank 6. The sibling demons repeatedly get the better of them, but our heroes show indomitable perseverance and defeat the demons at great cost. Meanwhile, the first death of an upper-rank demon in over a hundred years has an impact on the remaining upper-rank demons.

DEMON SLAYER

KIMETSU NO YAIBA

THE
UPPER
RANKS
GATHER

**KOYOHARU
GOTOUGE**

**DEMON SLAYER:
KIMETSU NO YAIBA
VOLUME 12**
Shonen Jump Edition

Story and Art by
KOYOHARU GOTOUGE

KIMETSU NO YAIBA
© 2016 by Koyoharu Gotouge
All rights reserved. First published in Japan
in 2016 by SHUEISHA Inc., Tokyo. English
translation rights arranged by SHUEISHA Inc.

TRANSLATION John Werry
ENGLISH ADAPTATION Stan!
TOUCH-UP ART & LETTERING John Hunt
DESIGN Jimmy Presler
EDITOR Mike Montesa

Printed in the U.S.A.

Published by VIZ Media, LLC
P.O. Box 77010
San Francisco, CA 94107

10 9 8 7 6 5 4 3 2 1
First printing, May 2020

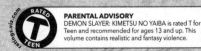

viz.com   shonenjump.com

*Flag: Thanks

*Back: Happy

KOYOHARU GOTOUGE

Hello! I'm Gotouge. I am truly thankful to everyone happy about the *Demon Slayer* anime as if it were their own good news! All the kind and congratulatory words, gifts and happiness massaged me and blew away my stiff shoulders and headaches. My nose is still running though. I'm sorry I can't reply individually or give you anything back. I'm blessed by much good fortune and the aid and encouragement of nice people helps a lot. I am always praying from the bottom of my heart for the health and happiness of people who are kind to me.